Contents

Some words are shown in bold, **like this**.
You can find them in the glossary on page 23.

What is a leopard seal?

A leopard seal is a **mammal** that spends most of its time on or near ice.

All mammals have some hair on their bodies and feed their babies milk.

Leopard seals live in freezing **polar** waters.

There are many different types of seal, but leopard seals are the strongest hunters.

What do leopard seals look like?

teeth

Leopard seals have teeth that are long and sharp.

These **predators** also have strong jaws.

clawed flipper

Leopard seals have thick spotted fur and clawed flippers.

Their spots make them look a bit like big cats called leopards!

Where do leopard seals live?

Antarctica

Leopard seals mainly live in or near **Antarctica**.

In Antarctica it is light all day and all night for part of the summer.

pack ice

In Antarctica it is dark all day and all night for part of the winter.

Antarctic seas are filled with large, cold chunks of moving ice called **pack ice**.

What do leopard seals do in the day?

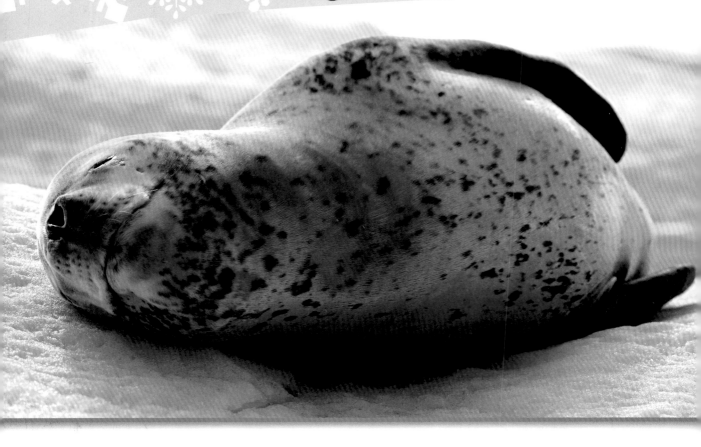

In the late summer and autumn, leopard seals often sleep until about midday.

They wake up after napping on **pack ice** and dive into the water to hunt.

penguin

Leopard seals are powerful hunters and fast swimmers.

They often wait near pack ice to catch penguins.

What do leopard seals eat?

penguin

Leopard seals eat **krill** and penguins.

Sometimes leopard seals even hunt other seals!

Many leopard seals also feed on fish and squid.

They get the water they need from the food they eat.

What hunts leopard seals?

killer whale

Not many animals hunt leopard seals.

Killer whales sometimes attack and eat them.

Leopard seals have to be extra careful during daylight hours.

Killer whales spot seals on **pack ice** and try to knock them into the water!

Do leopard seals live in groups?

Leopard seals do not usually live in groups.
They spend most of their time alone.

A mother leopard seal does not even stay with her baby for very long.

They only live together for about a month.

What do leopard seals do at night?

In the autumn and winter, leopard seals mainly hunt at night.

They dive into the water to hunt for food.

Leopard seals have excellent eyesight and a good sense of smell.

This helps them to find food in the dark.

What are baby leopard seals like?

pup

A mother seal gives birth to a baby seal about once a year.

Baby seals are called pups and they look like small versions of their parents.

The mother feeds her pup milk for three to four weeks.

Then young leopard seals are able to hunt and live alone!

Leopard seal body map

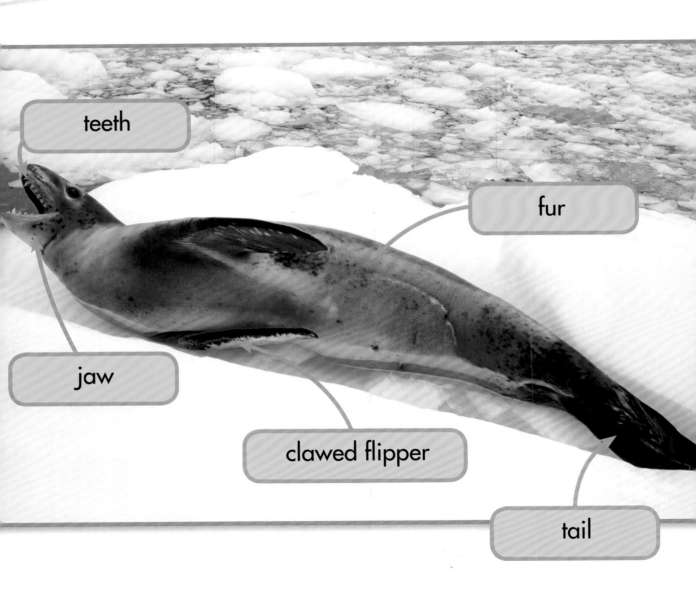

teeth

fur

jaw

clawed flipper

tail

Glossary

Antarctica very cold continent located at the South Pole

krill small shrimp-like animals

mammal animal that feeds its babies milk. All mammals have some hair or fur on their bodies.

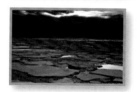

pack ice large chunks of moving ice

polar extremely cold areas at the top and bottom of the world

predator animal that hunts and kills other animals for food

Find out more

Books

Arctic and Antarctic (Eye Wonder), Lorie Mack (DK Publishing, 2006)
Seals, Christina Wilsdon (Gareth Stevens, 2010)

Websites

www.antarcticconnection.com/antarctic/wildlife/seals/leopard.shtml
Find out about leopard seals on the Antarctic Connection website.

www.nationalgeographic.com/coloringbook/leopardseals.html
National Geographic has information on leopard seals and a picture to colour.

Index